POPULAR SONGS

HAL LEONARD
TUDENT PIANO LIBRARY

Chart Hits

Arranged by Mona Rejino

CONTENTS

Cover Photo: © Deborah Roundtree / Getty Images

ISBN 978-1-4234-5200-3

7777 W. BLUEMOUND RD. P.O. BOX 13819 MILWAUKEE, WI 53213

Visit Hal Leonard Online at
www.halleonard.com

Bad Day

Words and Music by
Daniel Powter
Arranged by Mona Rejino

Moderate Groove ($\quad$ = 69)

Where is the mo - ment we need - ed the most?

You kick up the leaves _ and the mag - ic is lost. _

They tell me your blue skies fade to grey. They tell me your pas - sion's gone a -

way, and I don't need no car - ryin' on.

You stand in the line __ just to hit a new low. __

You're fak - in' the smile __ with the cof - fee to go. __

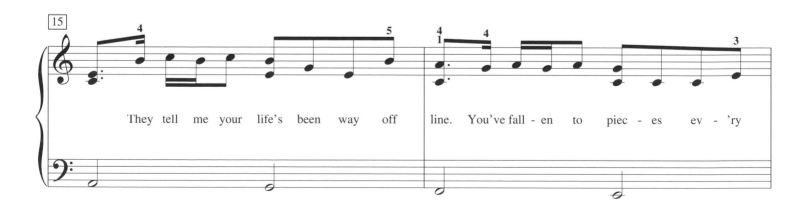

They tell me your life's been way off line. You've fall - en to piec - es ev - 'ry

4

time and I don't need no car - ryin' on be - cause you had a bad

cresc. *f*

day. You're tak - in' one down. You sing a sad song just to turn it a - round. You say you don't

know. You tell me don't lie. You work at a smile and you go for a ride. You had a bad

To Coda ⊕

day. The cam - 'ra don't lie. You're com - in' back down and you real - ly don't mind. You had a bad

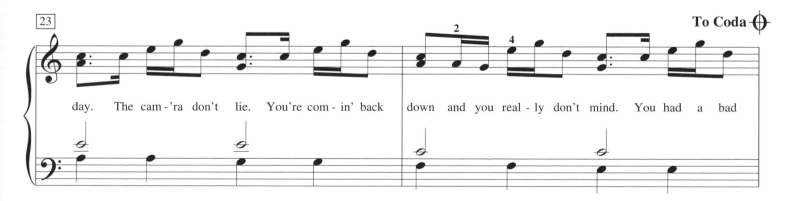

day. _____ You had a bad day.

Well, you need a blue sky hol - i -

mf

day. The point is they laugh at what you say and I don't need no car - ryin'

cresc.

on. _____ You had a bad

day. _____ Oh, _____

_____ on a hol-i-day. ____ Some-times the sys-tem goes on the blink and the

whole thing, it turns out wrong. You might not make it back and you know _ that you could

be well. Oh, that's strong _ and I'm not wrong, yeah. _____

7

So where is the pas - sion when you need it the most?

Oh, you and I. You kick up the leaves _ and the mag - ic is lost _

'cause you had a bad day. You're tak - in' one down. You sing a sad

song just to turn it a - round. You say you don't know. You tell me don't lie. You work at a

smile and you go for a ride. You had a bad day. You've seen what you like. And how does it

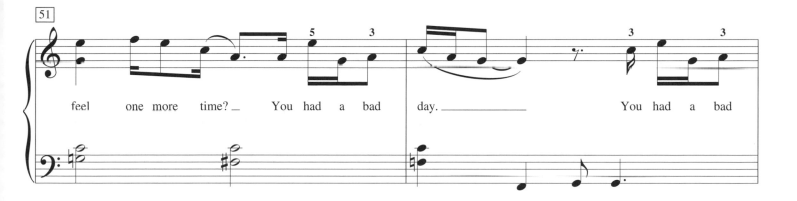

feel one more time? _ You had a bad day. _____ You had a bad

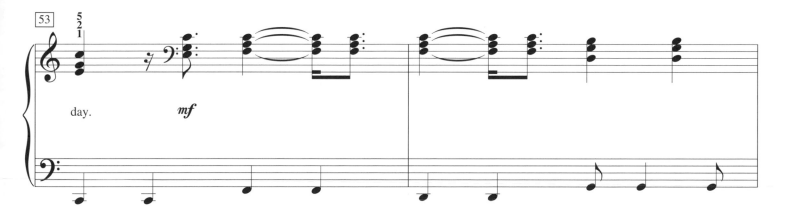

day. _ *mf*

mp *rit.*

Boston

Words and Music by Daniel Layus, Jared Palomar,
Josiah Rozencwajg and Justin South
Arranged by Mona Rejino

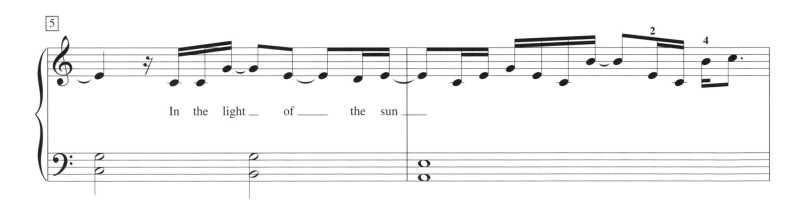

In the light of the sun

is there an - y - one?   Oh, it has be - gun.

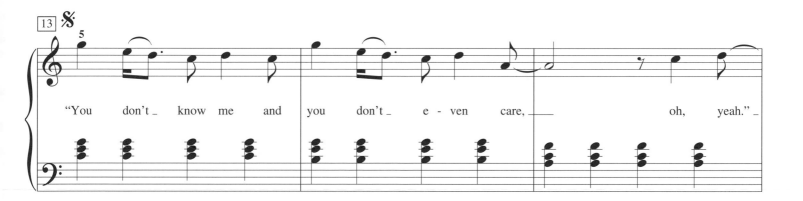

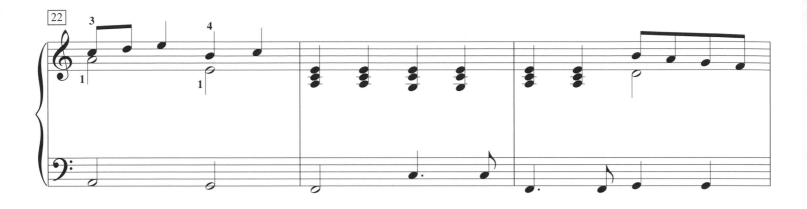

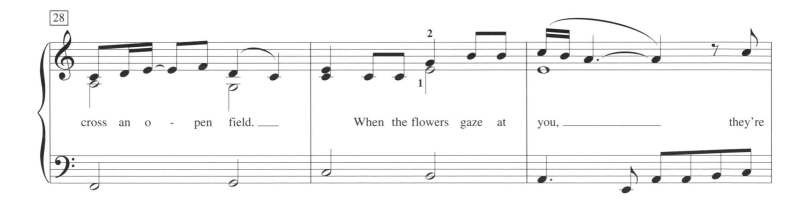

D.S. al Coda

not the on - ly ones   cry - in' when __ they see you. You said, _____

CODA

She said, "I think I'll   go to | Bos - ton. _____   I think I'll   start   a
cresc. | Bos - ton. _____   I think that   I'm   just

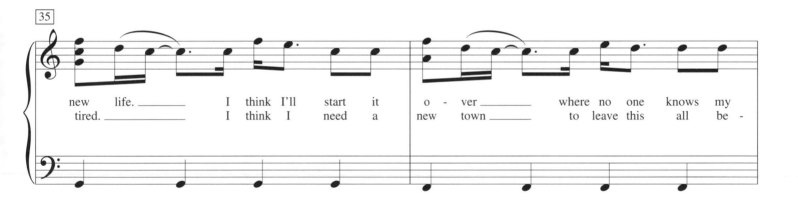

new life. _____   I think I'll   start   it | o - ver _____   where no one   knows   my
tired. _____   I think I   need   a | new town _____   to leave this   all   be -

name. __   I'll   get   out of   Cal - i - | for - nia. _____   I'm   tired   of   the
hind. __   I think I _____   need _____   a | sun - rise. _____   I'm   tired   of   the

weath - er.   I   think   I'll   get   a   lov - er____   and   fly   him   out   to
sun - set.   Hear   it's   nice   in   the   sum - mer,___   some   snow___ would   be

Spain. Oh, yeah, I think I'll go to   nice,_____ oh, yeah." ___ You don't_ know me and

you   don't _   e - ven   care,____   oh,   yeah.____

Bos - ton,   no one knows_ my   name._____

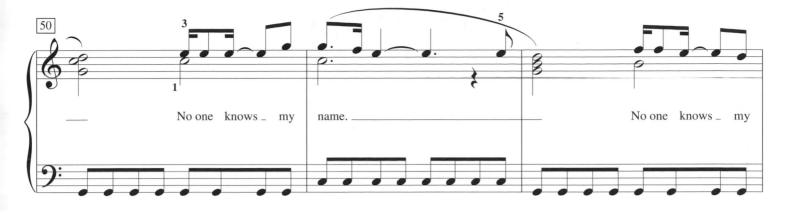

No one knows _ my name. _____ No one knows _ my

name. _____ *p*

No one knows _ my name. ____
rit.

15

Everything

Words and Music by Amy Foster-Gillies,
Michael Bublé and Alan Chang
Arranged by Mona Rejino

And you play it coy, but it's kind of cute. When you
And I can't be - lieve, oh, that I'm your man, and I

smile at me, you know ex - act - ly what you do. Ba - by, don't pre - tend that you don't know
get to kiss you, ba - by, just be - cause I can. What-ev - er comes our way, oh, we'll see

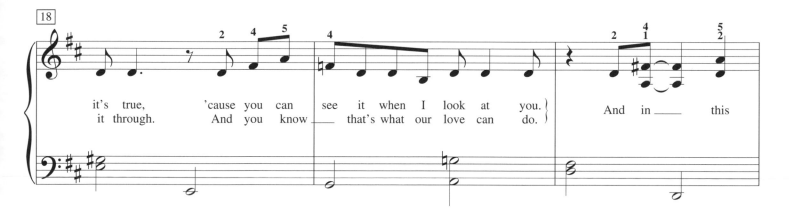

it's true, 'cause you can see it when I look at you.
it through. And you know that's what our love can do.

And in this

cra - zy life and through these cra - zy times,

it's you, ___ it's you. ___ You make me sing. ___ You're ev-'ry line, ___

dim. poco a poco

1.

you're ev-'ry word, ___ you're ev-'ry-thing. ___

mp

You're a car-

2.

you're ev-'ry-thing. ___

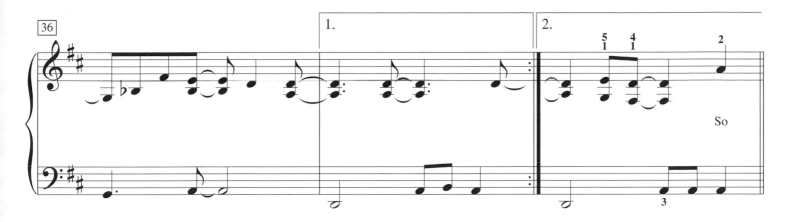

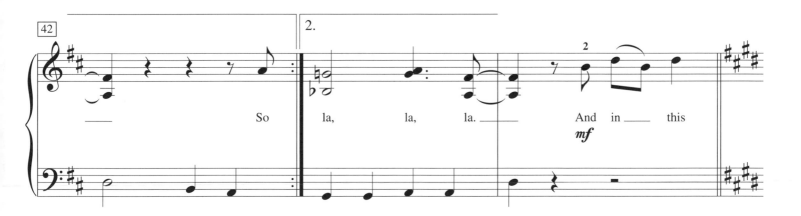

it's you, it's you. You make me sing. You're ev-'ry line,

you're ev-'ry word, you're ev-'ry-thing.

You're ev-'ry song,

mp

and I sing a-long 'cause you're my ev-'ry-thing.

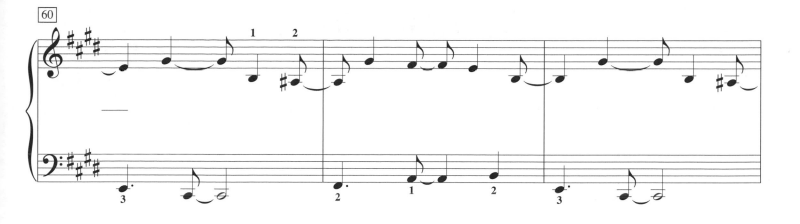

So la, la, la, la,

la, la, la. So la, la, _rit._

la, la, la, la, la, la, la, la, la.

February Song

Words by John Ondrasik and Josh Groban
Music by Josh Groban and Marius De Vries
Arranged by Mona Rejino

Moderately, in one (♩. = 48)

With pedal

Where has that ___ old   friend   gone,

lost in a Feb - ru - ar - y ___ song?   Tell him it

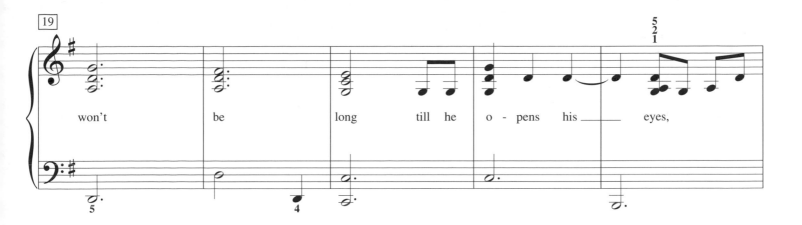

won't   be   long   till he o - pens his ___ eyes,

o - pens his ___ eyes.

Where is that ___ sim - ple

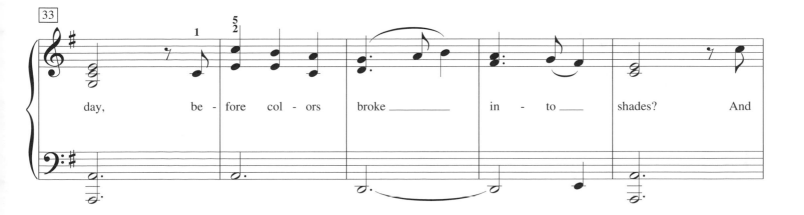

day,   be - fore col - ors broke ___ in - to ___ shades? And

how did I ___ ev - er fade in - to this ___

___ life, in - to this ___

___ life? And I nev - er ___

mf

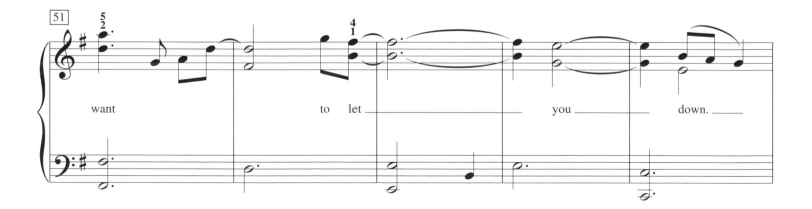

want to let ___ you ___ down. ___

For - give me if I _____

slip a - way. _____

When all that I've ___ known _____ is lost ___

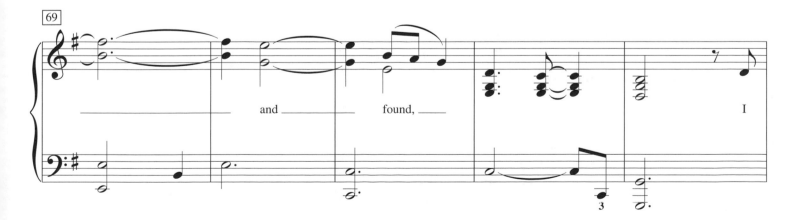

_____ and _____ found, _____ I

25

prom - ise you, I ____ I'll come ____ back to *dim.*

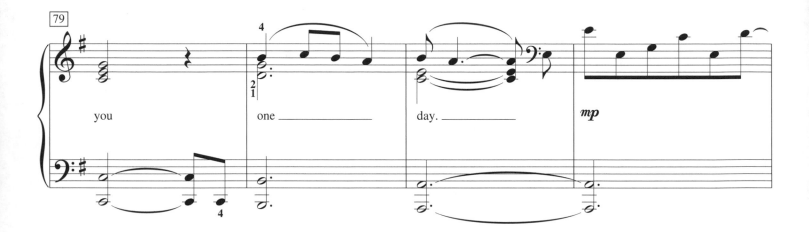

you one ____ day. ____ *mp*

Where has that ____ old

friend gone, lost in a Feb - ru - ar - y

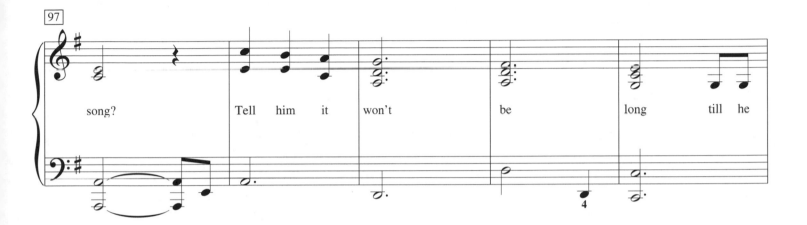

song? Tell him it won't be long till he

o - pens his eyes,

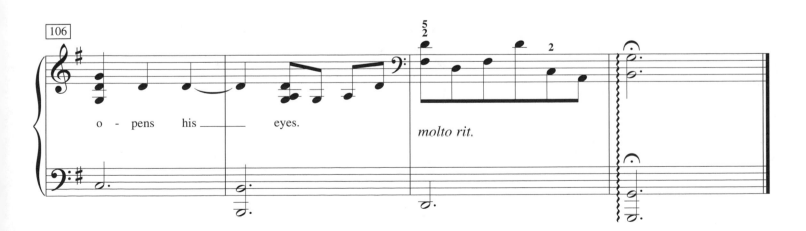

o - pens his eyes.

molto rit.

Home

Words and Music by
Chris Daughtry
Arranged by Mona Rejino

I'm star - in' out ___ in - to the night ___

___ try - ing to hide ___ the pain.

I'm go - in' to _____ the place where love and

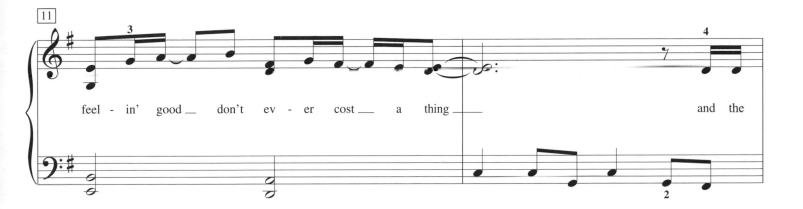

feel - in' good ___ don't ev - er cost ___ a thing _____ and the

pain you feel's __ a dif - f'rent kind of pain. _____

Well, I'm go - in' home, _ back to the place where I _____ be - long, _____ and where your

mf

love has al - ways been e - nough _ for me.

I'm not run - nin' from, _ no, I think you got _ me all wrong. I

don't re - gret _ this life I chose _ for me. _ But these

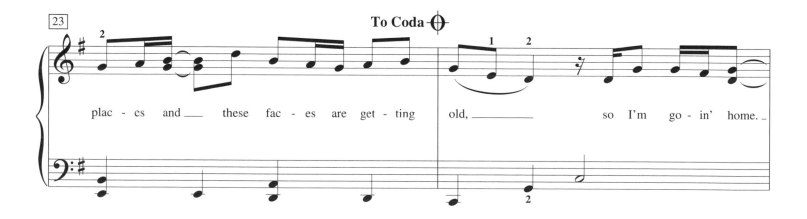

To Coda ⊕

plac - es and _ these fac - es are get - ting old, _ so I'm go - in' home. _

I've not al-ways been _ the best man or friend for you, but your love _ re-mains true _

_____ and I don't know why. You

al-ways seem to give _ me an-oth - er try. _

D.S. al Coda

CODA

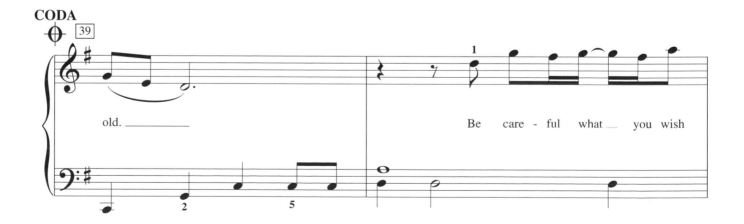

old. _____ Be care-ful what _ you wish

for, _____ 'cause you just might get it all. _____ You just might _ get it all _____

_____ and then some you don't want. _____ Be care - ful what _ you wish

for, _____ 'cause you just might _ get it all. _____ You just might _ get it all, _____

_____ yeah.

But these plac - es and __ these fac - es are get - ting

old. _____ I said, these plac - es and __ these fac - es are get - ting

old. _____ So I'm go - in' home. _____

I'm go - in' home. _____
mp

How to Save a Life

Words and Music by Joseph King
and Isaac Slade
Arranged by Mona Rejino

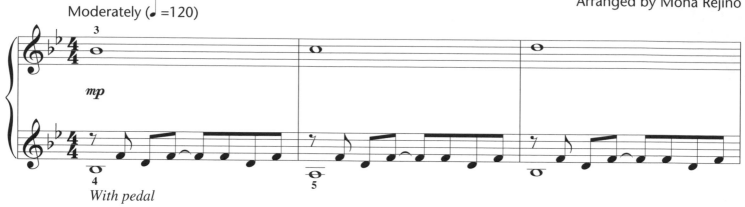

some sort of win - dow to your right, as he ___ goes

left and you ___ stay right. Be - tween ___ the lines ___

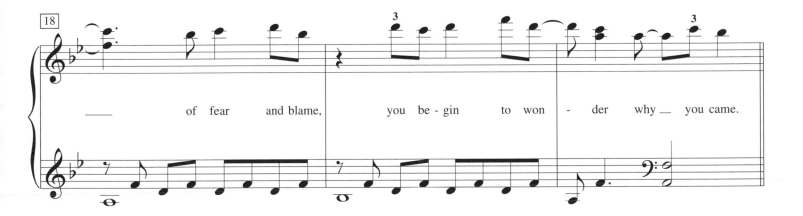

___ of fear and blame, you be - gin to won - der why ___ you came.

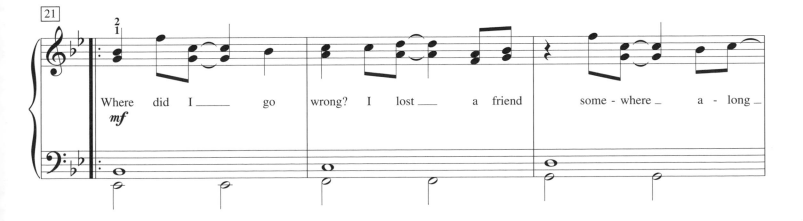

Where did I ___ go wrong? I lost ___ a friend some - where ___ a - long ___

_____ in the bit - ter - ness. And I would have _____ stayed up with you _____ all

night had I _____ known how to save _____ a life. _mp_

As

Let him know _____ that you _____ know best, 'cause
he be - gins _____ to raise _____ his voice, 'cause you

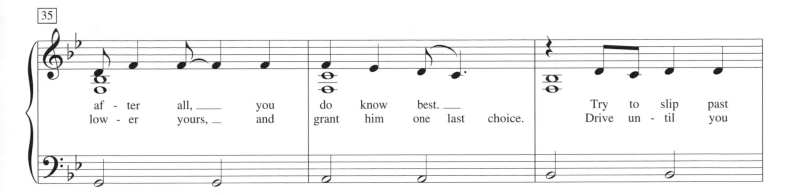

af - ter all, ____ you
low - er yours, _ and

do know best. ____
grant him one last choice.

Try to slip past
Drive un - til you

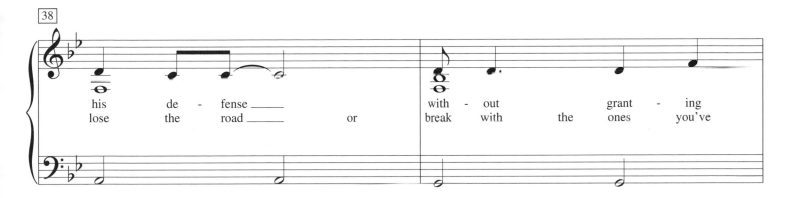

his de - fense ____
lose the road ____ or

with - out grant - ing
break with the ones you've

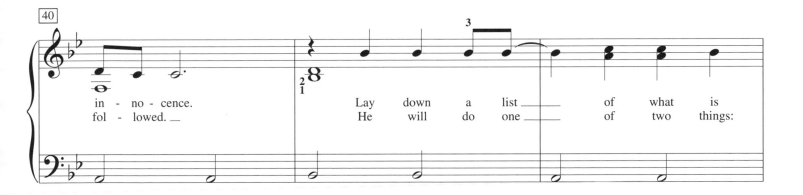

in - no - cence.
fol - lowed. _

Lay down a list ____ of what is
He will do one ____ of two things:

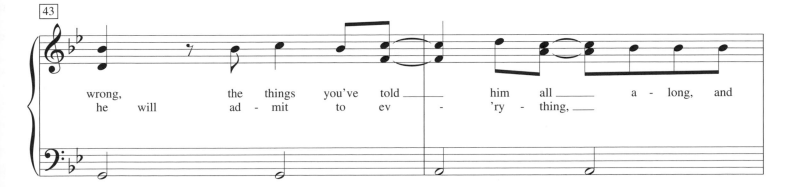

wrong, the things you've told ____ him all ____ a - long, and
he will ad - mit to ev - 'ry - thing, ____

pray to God _____ he hears _____ you, and
or he'll say he's he just not the same and

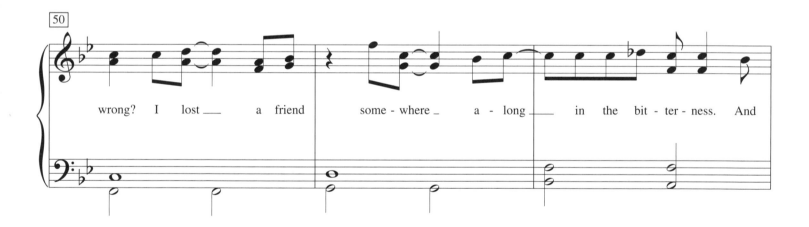

pray to God _____ he hears _____ you.
you'll be - gin _____ to won - der why you came. Where did I _____ go

mf

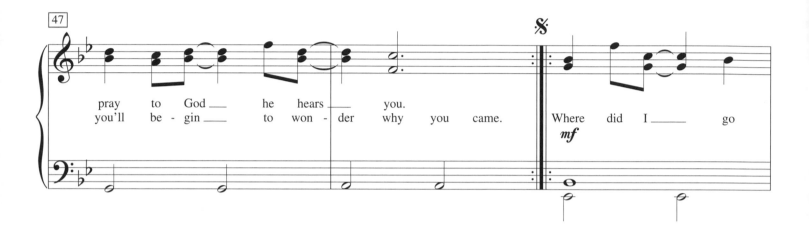

wrong? I lost _____ a friend some - where _ a - long _____ in the bit - ter - ness. And

I would have _____ stayed up with you _____ all night had I _____ known

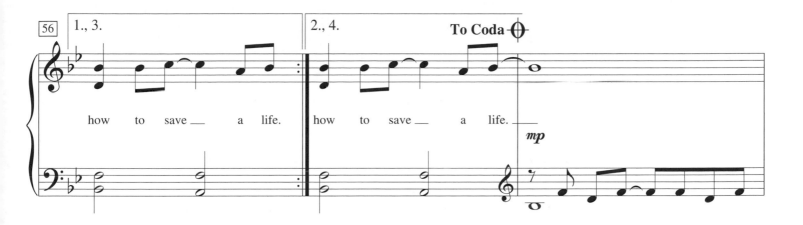

how to save ___ a life.   how to save ___ a life. ___

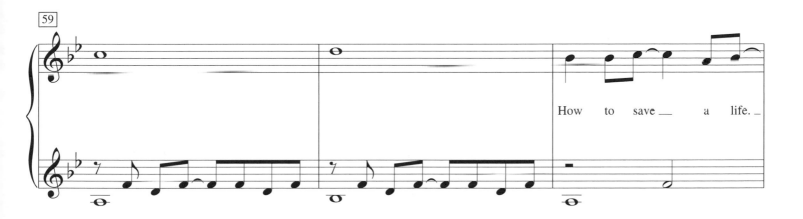

How to save ___ a life. ___

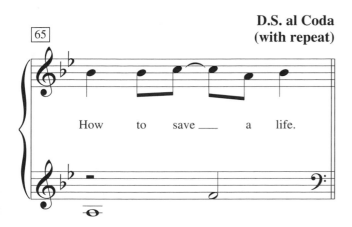

How to save ___ a life.

How to save ___ a life. __

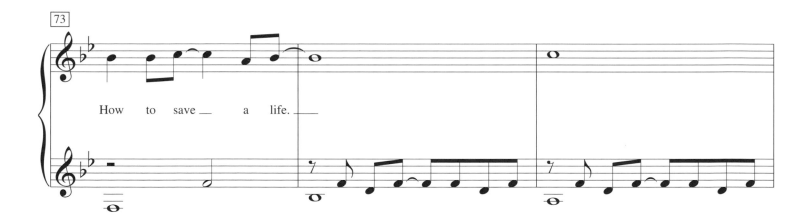

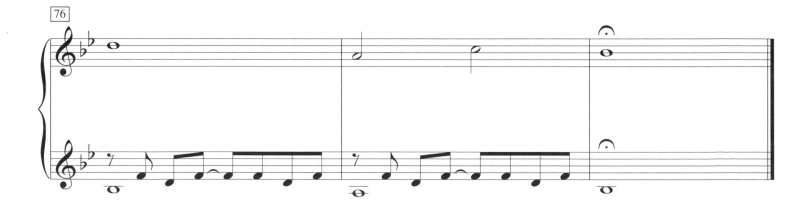

How to save ___ a life. ___

Put Your Records On

Words and Music by John Beck,
Steven Chrisanthou and Corinne Bailey Rae
Arranged by Mona Rejino

Moderately (♩ = 96)

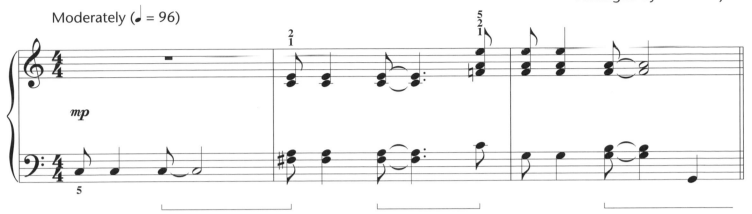

Three ____ lit - tle birds sat on my win - dow
Blue ____ as the sky, sun - burnt and lone - ly,

and they told me I don't need to wor - ry. ____
sip - pin' tea in a bar by the road - side. ____

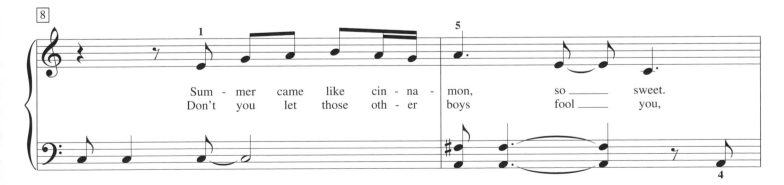

Sum - mer came like cin - na - mon, so ____ sweet.
Don't you let those oth - er boys fool ____ you,

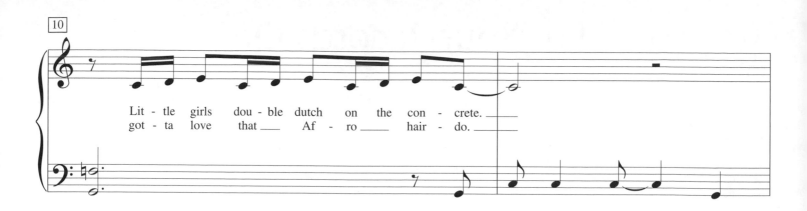

Tell me your fav -'rite song. __ You go a - head, let your hair __ down. __

Sap - phire and fad - ed jeans, __ I hope you get your dreams. __ Just go a - head, let your hair __

__ down. __ You're gon - na find your - self some - where, some - how. __

mp

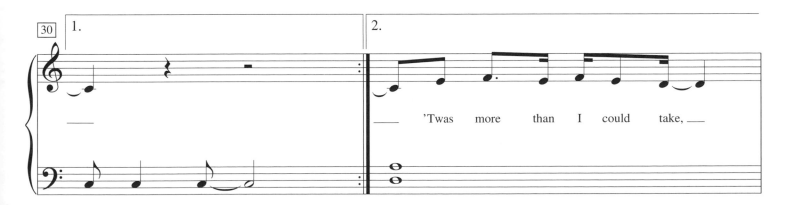

1.

2.

__ 'Twas more than I could take, __

pit - y for pit - y's sake. ___ Some nights kept me a - wake, ___

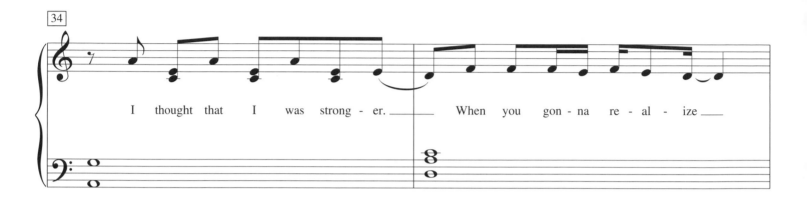

I thought that I was strong - er. ___ When you gon - na re - al - ize ___

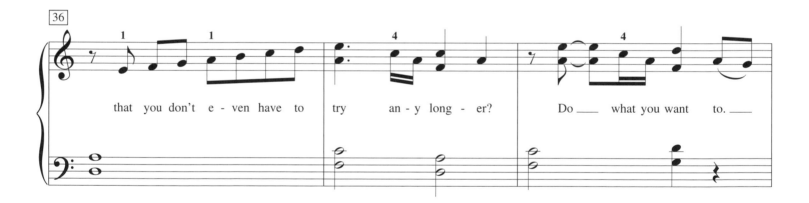

that you don't e - ven have to try an - y long - er? Do ___ what you want to. ___

Girl, put your rec - ords on. ___ Tell me your fav - 'rite song. ___

mf

What Hurts the Most

Words and Music by Steve Robson
and Jeffrey Steele
Arranged by Mona Rejino

Moderately slow (♩ = 69)

mf

With pedal

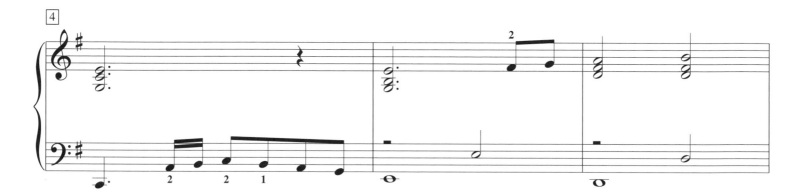

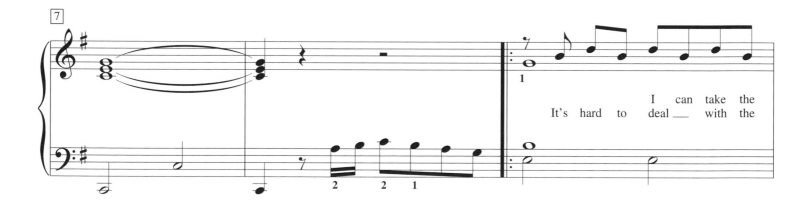

I can take the
It's hard to deal ___ with the

rain ___ on the roof of this emp-ty house, ___ that don't both-er me.
pain of los-in' you ev-'ry - where I go, ___ but I'm do-in' it.

I can take a few tears now and then and just let 'em out. _____
It's hard to force _____ that smile when I see our old friends and I'm a-lone.

I'm not a-fraid to cry, ev-'ry once in a while, e-ven though
Still hard-er get-tin' up, get-tin' dressed, liv-in' with this re-gret,

go-in' on with you gone still up-sets me. There are days ev-'ry now
but I know if I could do it o-ver, I would trade, give a-way

and a-gain I pre-tend I'm O. K., but that's _____ not what gets me.
all the words that I saved in my heart that I had nev-er spo-ken.

What hurts the most was be - in'

so _____ close and hav - in' so much to say

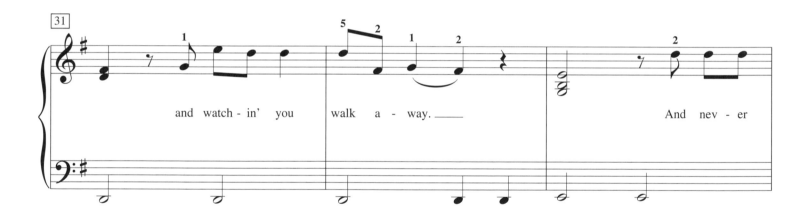

and watch - in' you walk a - way. _____ And nev - er

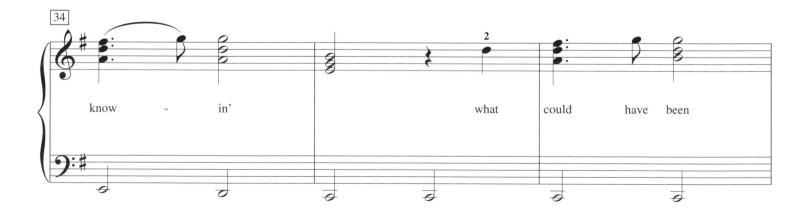

know - in' what could have been

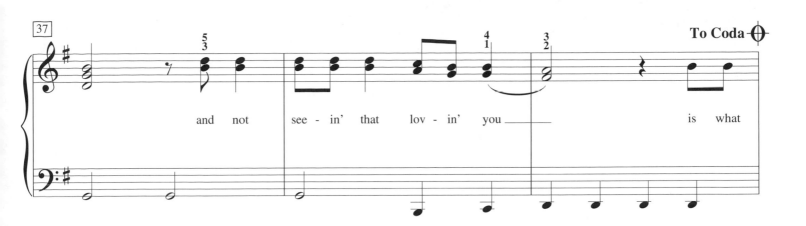

and not   see - in'   that   lov - in'   you ___   is   what

I   was   try'n' ___   to   do. ___

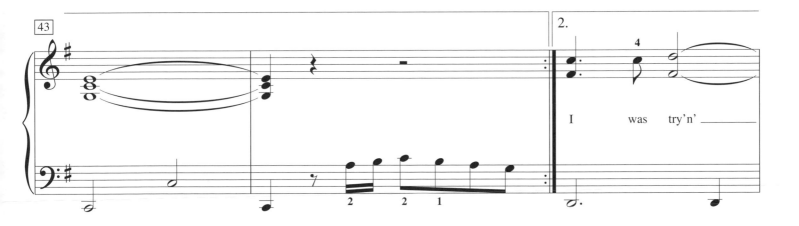

I   was   try'n' ___

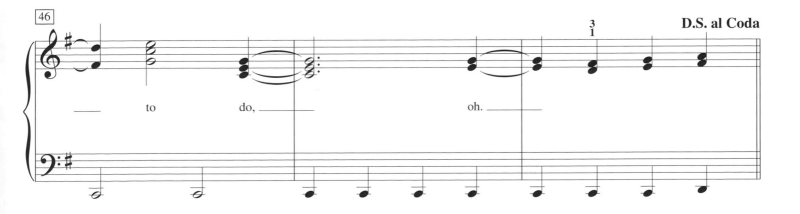

___   to   do, ___   oh. ___

I was try'n' to do. Not see - in' that lov - in' you,

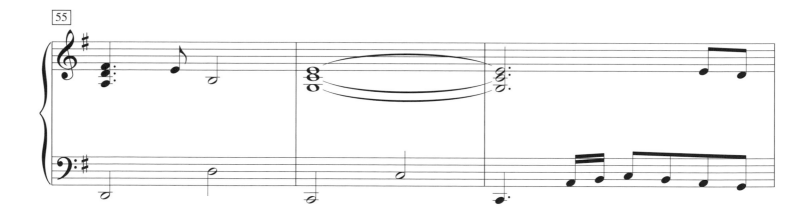

that's what I was try'n' to do.

rit.

COMPOSER SHOWCASE
HAL LEONARD STUDENT PIANO LIBRARY

This series showcases the varied talents of our **Hal Leonard Student Piano Library** family of composers.

Here is where you will find great original piano music by your favorite composers, including Phillip Keveren, Carol Klose, Jennifer Linn, Bill Boyd, and many others. Carefully graded for easy selection, each book contains gems that are certain to become tomorrow's classics!

EARLY ELEMENTARY

JAZZ PRELIMS
by Bill Boyd
HL00290032   12 Solos.......................$5.95

ELEMENTARY

JAZZ STARTERS I
by Bill Boyd
HL00290425   10 Solos.......................$6.95

LATE ELEMENTARY

CIRCUS SUITE
by Mona Rejino
HL00296665   5 Solos.......................$5.95

CORAL REEF SUITE
by Carol Klose
HL00296354   7 Solos.......................$5.95

JAZZ STARTERS II
by Bill Boyd
HL00290434   11 Solos.......................$6.95

JAZZ STARTERS III
by Bill Boyd
HL00290465   12 Solos.......................$6.95

LES PETITES IMAGES
by Jennifer Linn
HL00296664   7 Solos.......................$6.95

MOUSE ON A MIRROR
by Phillip Keveren
HL00296361   5 Solos.......................$6.95

PLAY THE BLUES!
by Luann Carman (Method Book)
HL00296357   10 Solos.......................$7.95

SHIFTY-EYED BLUES
by Phillip Keveren
HL00296374   5 Solos.......................$6.95

TEX-MEX REX
by Phillip Keveren
HL00296353   6 Solos.......................$5.95

FOR MORE INFORMATION, SEE YOUR LOCAL MUSIC DEALER, OR WRITE TO:

HAL•LEONARD® CORPORATION
7777 W. BLUEMOUND RD. P.O. BOX 13819 MILWAUKEE, WI 53213

EARLY INTERMEDIATE

CHRISTMAS FOR TWO
arr. Dan Fox (1 Piano, 4 Hands)
HL00290069   4 Medley Duets $6.95

DANCES FROM AROUND THE WORLD
by Christos Tsitsaros
HL00296688   7 Solos $6.95

EXPEDITIONS IN STYLE
by Bruce Berr
HL00296526   11 Solos.......................$6.95

EXPLORATIONS IN STYLE
by Bruce Berr
HL00290360   9 Solos.......................$6.95

FANCIFUL WALTZES
by Carol Klose
HL00296473   5 Solos $7.95

JAZZ BITS AND PIECES
by Bill Boyd
HL00290312   11 Solos.......................$6.95

MONDAY'S CHILD
by Deborah Brady
HL00296373   7 Solos.......................$6.95

PORTRAITS IN STYLE
by Mona Rejino
HL00296507   6 Solos.......................$6.95

THINK JAZZ!
by Bill Boyd (Method Book)
HL00290417.......................................$9.95

WORLD GEMS
arr. Amy O'Grady (Piano Ens./2 Pianos, 8 Hands)
HL00296505   6 Folk Songs $6.95

For full descriptions and song lists for the books listed here, and to view a complete list of titles in this series, please visit our website at www.halleonard.com

Prices, contents, & availability subject to change without notice.

INTERMEDIATE

AMERICAN IMPRESSIONS
by Jennifer Linn
HL00296471   6 Solos $7.95

CONCERTO FOR YOUNG PIANISTS
by Matthew Edwards (2 Pianos, 4 Hands)
HL00296356 Book/CD.......................$16.95

DAKOTA DAYS
by Sondra Clark
HL00296521   5 Solos.......................$6.95

DESERT SUITE
by Carol Klose
HL00296667   6 Solos.......................$6.95

ISLAND DELIGHTS
by Sondra Clark
HL00296666   4 Solos.......................$6.95

JAMBALAYA
by Eugénie Rocherolle (2 Pianos, 8 Hands)
HL00296654   Piano Ensemble............$9.95

JAZZ DELIGHTS
by Bill Boyd
HL00240435   11 Solos.......................$6.95

JAZZ FEST
by Bill Boyd
HL00240436   10 Solos.......................$6.95

JAZZ SKETCHES
by Bill Boyd
HL00220001   8 Solos.......................$6.95

LES PETITES IMPRESSIONS
by Jennifer Linn
HL00296355   6 Solos.......................$6.95

POETIC MOMENTS
by Christos Tsitsaros
HL00296403   8 Solos.......................$7.95

ROMP!
by Phillip Keveren
(Digital Ensemble/6 Keyboards, 6 Players)
HL00296549   Book/CD.......................$9.95
HL00296548   Book/GM Disk $9.95

SONGS WITHOUT WORDS
by Christos Tsitsaros
HL00296506   9 Solos.......................$7.95

THREE ODD METERS
by Sondra Clark (1 Piano, 4 Hands)
HL00296472   3 Duets $6.95

The Hal Leonard Student Piano Library has great songs, and you will find all your favorites here: Disney classics, Broadway and movie favorites, and today's top hits. These graded collections are skillfully and imaginatively arranged for students and pianists at every level, from elementary solos with teacher accompaniments to sophisticated piano solos for the advancing pianist.

The Beatles
arr. Eugénie Rocherolle
Intermediate piano solos. Songs: *Can't Buy Me Love • Get Back • Here Comes the Sun • Martha My Dear • Michelle • Ob-La-Di, Ob-La-Da • Revolution • Yesterday.*
Correlates with HLSPL Level 5.
00296649..$9.95

Broadway Hits
arr. Carol Klose
Early-intermediate/intermediate piano solos. Songs: *Beauty and the Beast • Circle of Life • Do-Re-Mi • It's a Grand Night for Singing • The Music of the Night • Tomorrow • Where Is Love? • You'll Never Walk Alone.*
Correlates with HLSPL Levels 4/5.
00296650..$6.95

Christmas Cheer
arr. Phillip Keveren
Early intermediate level. For 1 Piano/4 Hands. Songs: *Caroling, Caroling • The Christmas Song • It Must Have Been the Mistletoe • It's Beginning to Look like Christmas • Rudolph the Red-Nosed Reindeer • You're All I Want for Christmas.*
Correlates with HLSPL Level 4.
00296616..$6.95

Christmas Time Is Here
arr. Eugénie Rocherolle
Intermediate level. For 1 piano/4 hands. Songs: *Christmas Time Is Here • Feliz Navidad • Here Comes Santa Claus (Right Down Santa Claus Lane) • I'll Be Home for Christmas • Little Saint Nick • White Christmas.*
Correlates with HLSPL Level 5.
00296614..$6.95

Disney Favorites
arr. Phillip Keveren
Late-elementary/early-intermediate piano solos. Songs: *Beauty and the Beast • Circle of Life • A Dream Is a Wish Your Heart Makes • I'm Late; Little April Shower • A Whole New World (Aladdin's Theme) • You Can Fly! • You'll Be in My Heart.*
Correlates with HLSPL Levels 3/4.
00296647..$9.95

Disney characters and artwork © Disney Enterprises, Inc.

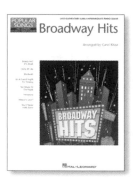

Getting to Know You – Rodgers & Hammerstein Favorites
Illustrated music book. Elementary/late elementary piano solos with teacher accompaniments. Songs: *Bali H'ai • Dites-Moi (Tell Me Why) • The Farmer and the Cowman • Getting to Know You • Happy Talk • I Whistle a Happy Tune • I'm Gonna Wash That Man Right Outa My Hair • If I Loved You • Oh, What a Beautiful Mornin' • Oklahoma • Shall We Dance? • Some Enchanted Evening • The Surrey with the Fringe on Top.*
Correlates with HLSPL Level 3
00296613..$12.95

Movie Favorites
arr. Fred Kern
Early-intermediate/intermediate piano solos. Songs: *Forrest Gump* (Feather Theme) *• Hakuna Matata • My Favorite Things • My Heart Will Go On • The Phantom of the Opera • Puttin' On the Ritz • Stand by Me.*
Correlates with HLSPL Levels 4/5.
00296648..$6.95

Sounds of Christmas (Volume 3)
arr. Rosemary Barrett Byers
Late elementary/early intermediate level. For 1 piano/4 hands. Songs: *Blue Christmas • Christmas Is A-Comin' (May God Bless You) • I Saw Mommy Kissing Santa Claus • Merry Christmas, Darling • Shake Me I Rattle (Squeeze Me I Cry) • Silver Bells.*
Correlates with HLSPL Levels 3/4.
00296615..$6.95

Today's Hits
arr. Mona Rejino
Intermediate-level piano solos. Songs: *Bless the Broken Road • Breakaway • Don't Know Why • Drops of Jupiter (Tell Me) • Home • Listen to Your Heart • She Will Be Loved • A Thousand Miles.*
Correlates with HLSPL Level 5.
00296646..$6.95

You Raise Me Up
arr. Deborah Brady
Contemporary Christian favorites. Elementary-level arrangements. Optional teacher accompaniments add harmonic richness. Songs: *All I Need • Forever • Open the Eyes of My Heart, Lord • We Bow Down • You Are So Good to Me • You Raise Me Up.*
Correlates with HLSPL Levels 2/3.
00296576..$7.95

Prices, contents and availability subject to change without notice. Prices may vary outside the U.S.

Visit our web site at
www.halleonard.com/hlspl.jsp
for all the newest titles in this series and other books in the Hal Leonard Student Piano Library.

FOR MORE INFORMATION, SEE YOUR LOCAL MUSIC DEALER, OR WRITE TO:

HAL•LEONARD®
CORPORATION
7777 W. BLUEMOUND RD. P.O. BOX 13819 MILWAUKEE, WI 53213